My Neighbour Totoro

Adapted by Tom Morton-Smith

T0021666

methuen | drama

LONDON · NEW YORK · OXFORD · NEW DELHI · SYDNEY

METHUEN DRAMA
Bloomsbury Publishing Plc
50 Bedford Square, London, WC1B 3DP, UK
1385 Broadway, New York, NY 10018, USA
29 Earlsfort Terrace, Dublin 2, Ireland

BLOOMSBURY, METHUEN DRAMA and the Methuen
Drama logo are trademarks of Bloomsbury Publishing Plc

First published in Great Britain 2024

A catalogue record for this book is available from the British Library.

A catalog record for this book is available from the Library of Congress.

ISBN: PB: 978-1-3504-4867-4
ePDF: 978-1-3504-4869-8
eBook: 978-1-3504-4868-1

Series: Modern Plays

Typeset by Mark Heslington Ltd, Scarborough, North Yorkshire
Printed and bound in Great Britain

To find out more about our authors and books visit
www.bloomsbury.com and sign up for our newsletters.

THE ROYAL SHAKESPEARE COMPANY

The Shakespeare Memorial Theatre was founded by Charles Flower, a local brewer, and opened in Stratford-upon-Avon in 1879. Since then, the plays of Shakespeare have been performed here, alongside the work of his contemporaries and of current contemporary playwrights. In 1960, the Royal Shakespeare Company as we now know it was formed by Peter Hall and Fordham Flower. The founding principles were threefold: the Company would embrace the freedom and power of Shakespeare's work, train and develop young actors and directors and, crucially, experiment in new ways of making theatre. The RSC quickly became known for exhilarating performances of Shakespeare alongside new masterpieces such as *The Homecoming* and *Old Times* by Harold Pinter. It was a combination that thrilled audiences, and this close and exacting relationship between writers from different eras has become the fuel that powers the creativity of the RSC.

In 1974, The Other Place opened in a tin hut on Waterside under the visionary leadership and artistic directorship of Buzz Goodbody. Determined to explore Shakespeare's plays in intimate proximity to her audience and to make small-scale, radical new work, Buzz revitalised the Company's interrogation between the contemporary and classical repertoire. This was followed by the founding of the Swan Theatre in 1986 – a space dedicated to Shakespeare's contemporaries, as well as later plays from the Restoration period, alongside living writers.

In nearly 60 years of producing new plays, we have collaborated with some of the most exciting writers of their generation. These have included: Edward Albee, Howard Barker, Alice Birch, Richard Bean, Edward Bond, Howard Brenton, Marina Carr, Lolita Chakrabarti, Caryl Churchill, Martin Crimp, Can Dündar, David Edgar, Helen Edmundson, James Fenton, Georgia Fitch, Robin French, Juliet Gilkes Romero, Fraser Grace, David Greig, Tanika Gupta, Matt Hartley, Ella Hickson, Kirsty Housley, Dennis Kelly, Hannah Khalil, Anders Lustgarten, Tarell Alvin McCraney, Martin McDonagh, Tom Morton-Smith, Rona Munro, Richard Nelson, Anthony Neilson, Harold Pinter, Phil Porter, Mike Poulton, Mark Ravenhill, Somalia Seaton, Adriano Shaplin, Tom Stoppard, debbie tucker green, Frances Ya-Chu Cowhig, Timberlake Wertenbaker, Peter Whelan and Roy Williams.

The RSC is committed to illuminating the relevance of Shakespeare's plays and the works of his contemporaries for the next generation of audiences and believes that our continued investment in new plays and living writers is an essential part of that mission.

Support us and make a difference
For more information visit **www.rsc.org.uk/support**

Miranda Curtis CMG – Lead Production Supporter of *My Neighbour Totoro*

The RSC Acting Companies are generously supported by The Gatsby Charitable Foundation

New Work at the RSC is generously supported by Hawthornden Foundation and The Drue and H.J. Heinz II Charitable Trust

Supported using public funding by
ARTS COUNCIL ENGLAND

STUDIO GHIBLI

Studio Ghibli was founded in 1985 by animated film directors Isao Takahata and Hayao Miyazaki and has produced 25 feature-length films. The Studio's *Spirited Away* (2001), *Howl's Moving Castle* (2004) and *Princess Mononoke* (1997) are among Japan's top 10 grossing films.

Studio Ghibli films have garnered numerous awards and critical acclaim from film critics and animation specialists around the world. *Spirited Away* was awarded the Golden Bear as the Best Feature Film at the 2002 Berlin International Film Festival and won the 2002 Academy Awards for Best Animated Feature Film. In October 2001, Studio Ghibli, in conjunction with The Tokuma Memorial Cultural Foundation for Animation, founded the Ghibli Museum, Mitaka, designed by Hayao Miyazaki.

The Wind Rises (2013), *The Tale of The Princess Kaguya* (2013), *When Marnie Was There* (2014) and *The Red Turtle* (2016) have earned the studio four consecutive nominations for the Academy Awards for Best Animated Feature Film. *Earwig and the Witch* (2020) was an official selection for the 2020 Cannes Film Festival. The studio's latest film, *The Boy and the Heron,* was released in Japan on 14 July 2023.

IMPROBABLE

Led by Phelim McDermott and Lee Simpson, Improbable is an award-winning theatre company that defies categorisation. At the heart of our artistic practice is improvisation. Whether in performance, rehearsal or development, the practice and philosophy of improvisation is at the core of our creation process.

The breadth of Improbable's experience is unrivalled and we occupy a vital space in the landscape of UK and international theatre, working with a huge range of partners nationally and internationally across sectors and scales. Other recent on-stage collaborations and projects have included: *The Hours,* Metropolitan Opera; *Akhnaten* (Olivier Award winner for Best Opera Production, Grammy Award for Best Opera Recording), English National Opera; *Perfect Show for Rachel* created by Zoo Co at Barbican (winner Off West End Award, Access); *An Improbable Musical,* Royal & Derngate, Northampton; *Tao Of Glass,* with Factory International, Perth Festival, Ruhrfestspiele Recklinghausen, Hong Kong New Vision Arts Festival and Carolina Performing Arts – University of North Carolina at Chapel Hill in association with Naomi Milgrom AO. We were awarded Producer of the Year at The Stage Awards in 2023.

Beyond our work on stage, we use Open Space Technology to create and hold diverse and deeply democratic spaces that bring communities together to work on urgent issues. We do this for the theatre sector through our Devoted & Disgruntled programme and work with other sectors and organisations through Open Space For Hire and Improbable For Business. Improbable is a core supporter of M/Others Who Make, an international network for women and non-binary people who care about creating, and create whilst caring.

NIPPON TV

Nippon Television Holdings, Inc. is a media and content company whose core operation is broadcasting. At the nucleus of its businesses is the subsidiary Nippon Television Network Corporation, Japan's first commercial television broadcaster that hit the airwaves in 1953. Celebrating its 70th anniversary this year (2023), the country's leading linear platform enjoys widespread support from viewers, propelling it to win the annual Triple Crown Title for the 11th consecutive year in 2021 by ranking No. 1 in individual viewer ratings across all three timeslot categories. In October 2023, NIPPON TV acquired the shares of Studio Ghibli, making it a subsidiary. As part of the same group, NIPPON TV continues to support Studio Ghibli.

Studio Ghibli's *My Neighbour Totoro* was first performed at the Barbican, London on 8 October 2022, presented by Joe Hisaishi and the Royal Shakespeare Company in collaboration with Nippon TV and Improbable. The revival of the production opened at the Barbican, London on 21 November 2023. The cast was as follows:

KANTA	**KA LONG KELVIN CHAN**	陳嘉朗
HIROSHI	**ANDREW FUTAISHI**	二石アンドリュー
MISS HARA	**ARINA II**	伊井 杏里那
MEI	**MEI MAC**	麥美玲
NURSE EMIKO	**AMANDA MAUD**	
KAZE NO KOE / SINGER　風の声	**AI NINOMIYA**	二宮 愛
SATSUKI	**AMI OKUMURA JONES**	奥村 英衣未
YASUKO	**EMILY PIGGFORD**	
TATSUO	**DAI TABUCHI**	田渕 大
GRANNY OGAKI	**JACQUELINE TATE**	藤井 夢華
TSUKIKO	**NAOMI YANG**	杨易尘
KAZEGO PUPPETEERS　風子	**JESSIE BAEK**	백은재 / 白恩才
	KA LONG KELVIN CHAN	
	JASMINE CHIU	趙明
	ELIZABETH CHU	朱迦希
	ANDREW FUTAISHI	
	YOJIRO ICHIKAWA	市川 洋二郎
	ARINA II	
	ANNA KATO	加藤 安奈
	MATTHEW LEONHART	布文龍
	AMANDA MAUD	
	YUKI NITTA	新田悠基
	BRIGHT ONG	王泽伟
	MARK TAKESHI OTA	太田マーク武
	EMILY PIGGFORD	
	SI RAWLINSON	楊世朗
	GUN SUEN	孫志鴻
	DAI TABUCHI	
	JACQUELINE TATE	
	SHAOFAN WILSON	金小凡
	NAOMI YANG	
SWING KAZEGO PUPPETEERS	**JASMINE BAYES**	
	BOAZ CHAD	陳政樺
	HEATHER LAI	黎曉瑩
	DANIEL PHUNG	周潤發

All other parts played by members of the Company.

CREATIVES

MUSIC BY	JOE HISAISHI
ADAPTED BY	TOM MORTON-SMITH
FROM THE FEATURE ANIMATION BY	HAYAO MIYAZAKI
DIRECTOR	PHELIM McDERMOTT
PRODUCTION DESIGNER	TOM PYE
PUPPETRY DESIGNER & DIRECTOR	BASIL TWIST
COSTUME DESIGNER	KIMIE NAKANO 中野 希美江
LIGHTING DESIGNER	JESSICA HUNG HAN YUN
ORCHESTRATOR AND ARRANGER	WILL STUART
SOUND DESIGNER	TONY GAYLE
MOVEMENT DIRECTOR	YOU-RI YAMANAKA 山中 結莉
VIDEO DESIGNERS	FINN ROSS
	ANDREA SCOTT
DRAMATURG	PIPPA HILL
CASTING DIRECTOR	HANNAH MILLER CDG
SOUND EFFECTS & SOUNDSCAPE DESIGNER	NICOLA T. CHANG 張彤
MUSIC SUPERVISOR	BRUCE O'NEIL
ORCHESTRAL MANAGER	DAVID GALLAGHER
MUSIC DIRECTOR	MATT SMITH
ASSOCIATE DIRECTOR	AILIN CONANT コナント愛林
PUPPETRY ASSOCIATE	MERVYN MILLAR
ASSOCIATE SET DESIGNER	ISOBEL NICOLSON
ASSOCIATE LIGHTING DESIGNER & PROGRAMMER	TAMYKHA PATTERSON
ASSOCIATE SOUND DESIGNER	STEVEN ATKINSON
CASTING ASSOCIATE	MARTIN POILE
VIDEO ASSOCIATE	BARBORA ŠENOLTOVÁ
VOICE COACH	JENRU WANG 王眞如
CREATIVE COLLABORATORS	IMPROBABLE
ENGLISH LYRICS	TOM MORTON-SMITH
LITERAL LYRICS TRANSLATION	JO ALLAN
PRODUCTION MANAGER	JAMIE MAISEY
RESIDENT DIRECTOR	ISKANDAR اردنكس
	R. SHARAZUDDIN 伊斯干达
COMPANY MANAGER	ROBIN LONGLEY
STAGE MANAGER	SARAH ASKEW
DEPUTY STAGE MANAGER	MORAG LAVERY
ASSISTANT STAGE MANAGERS	GEORGINA PEAD
	LAURA SMITH
	CHARLI UNWIN

CREATIVE PRODUCTION INTERPRETER	**SHUKO NOGUCHI**
PRODUCER NTV	**KENICHI YODA**
LINE PRODUCER NTV	**HISASHI IGARASHI**
ASSISTANT PRODUCER NTV	**AYUMI SHIRAI**
PRODUCTION COORDINATOR	**TOM DICKINSON**
GENERAL MANAGER	**REBECCA TREANOR**
EXECUTIVE PRODUCER	**GRISELDA YORKE**
EXECUTIVE PRODUCER	**JOE HISAISHI**

MUSICIANS

MUSIC DIRECTOR/KEYBOARD	**MATT SMITH**
CLARINET/BASS CLARINET/ ALTO SAXOPHONE/WHISTLE	**CLAIRE McINERNEY**
TRUMPET/FLUGELHORN/ PICCOLO TRUMPET	**CHRIS AVISON**
TROMBONE/EUPHONIUM	**EMMA JULIETTE HODGSON**
VIOLIN/TUBULAR BELL	**TAKANE FUNATSU** 船津たかね
CELLO/TUBULAR BELL	**DAVINA SHUM** 岑睿
ELECTRIC GUITAR/STEEL STRING/ ACOUSTIC GUITAR/MANDOLIN	**ALEX 明 CRAWFORD**
DOUBLE BASS/BASS GUITAR/KEYBOARD	**RORY DEMPSEY**
DRUM KIT/PERCUSSION	**JAMES TURNER**
PERCUSSION	**JOANNE CHIANG** 蔣蕎安
ASSISTANT MUSIC DIRECTOR & COVER CONDUCTOR	**AMY HSU** 許淳安

This text may differ slightly from the play as performed.
Company and creative listing as at opening night, 2023.

Thanks first and foremost to Hayao Miyazaki, Joe Hisaishi and Toshio Suzuki for their confidence and blessing – and that thanks extends to all at Studio Ghibli and Nippon TV for their help in bringing this project into the world. Thanks especially to Kenichi Yoda and Hisashi Igarashi for their support, advice and rigour (and the occasional Japanese lesson). Thank you to Phelim McDermott and all at Improbable for their collaboration, openness and friendship. To Pippa Hill, Réjane Collard-Walker and the rest of the RSC's literary department – not only for their dramaturgy but for the technical and detailed contractual work behind the scenes. Huge thanks to Griselda Yorke, Rebecca Treanor, Miranda Curtis and all at the RSC. Thank you to all the creatives, creators, actors, puppeteers and technicians who have contributed to the many script readings and workshops, and to the incredible casts and crews that assembled to bring this show to life in both 2022 and 2023. Thank you to Shuko Noguchi, Erica Whyman, Kevin Fitzmaurice, Rose Cobbe and Kumiko Mendl. And gratitude beyond measure to Jen Tan – the fiercest, most powerful constant I could hope to have in my life.

Tom Morton-Smith
January 2024

My Neighbour Totoro

for my daughter

Characters

Satsuki Kusakabe
Mei Kusakabe
Tatsuo Kusakabe
Yasuko Kusakabe

Kanta Ogaki
Granny Ogaki
Hiroshi Ogaki
Tsukiko Ogaki

Nurse Emiko
Miss Hara

Ōtotoro
Chōtotoro
Shōtotoro

Removal Man
Workers
Bus Driver
Postman
Farmer
Man
Woman
Villagers

Soot-Sprites
Catbus

1955. Matsugo – a small farming community on the outskirts of Tokyo.

Act One

Song: 'Hey, Let's Go'.

1 – The Village in May

The Kusakabe family – **Tatsuo**, **Satsuki** *and* **Mei** *– arrive in a small, three-wheeled tuktuk truck driven by a* **Removal Man**. *It is moving day and the truck is overflowing with furniture and suitcases.*

Mei *and* **Satsuki** *peek out of the back between pieces of furniture.*

Tatsuo　How are you doing back there?

Mei　Would you like a toffee?

Tatsuo　No thank you, Mei – not for me. How are you doing, Satsuki?

Satsuki　I'm a bit squashed.

Tatsuo　We're nearly there – not much longer now.

A **Postman** *rides by on a bicycle.*

Mei　Would you like a toffee?

The **Postman** *loses control of his bicycle and nearly crashes.*

They come to a stop. **Tatsuo** *steps out of the cab – he is a little lost. He turns a map around in his hands – trying to get his bearings.* **Satsuki** *and* **Mei** *climb out of the truck.*

Tatsuo　Perhaps we should have taken that turning . . .?

Mei　Dad!

Tatsuo　Yes, Mei?

Mei　Are we lost?

Tatsuo　Not lost . . . just *unfamiliar* . . .

Kanta *is watching them from a distance.* **Satsuki** *sees him.*

Satsuki   Hello.

Kanta *turns to run but is blocked by his parents –* **Hiroshi** *and* **Tsukiko Ogaki**.

Hiroshi   Are you having some trouble there?

Tatsuo   Sorry . . . yes . . . just a little misplaced. We're new to the area.

Tsukiko   You must be Professor Kusakabe. I'm Tsukiko Ogaki . . . we've corresponded several times.

Tatsuo   Yes! Of course! A pleasure to finally meet you.

Hiroshi   You must be the new neighbours!

Tatsuo   Tatsuo . . . and this is Satsuki, my eldest . . . and this is Mei.

Mei   I'm four years old.

Hiroshi   Hiroshi. I am thirty-seven.

Tsukiko   And this is our son, Kanta. Kanta . . .?

Kanta *has disappeared behind the truck.* **Mei** *finds him and drags him unwillingly into view.*

Mei   Here he is!

Hiroshi (*looking over the truck*)   Not exactly travelling light, are you?

Tatsuo   It's mostly books.

Hiroshi   If you need a hand . . . I've got a strong back . . . a good pair of arms.

Tatsuo   Very kind but we have our removal man . . . we should be fine.

The **Removal Man** *waves.*

Hiroshi   If there is anything we can do to help – do not hesitate to call.

Tatsuo   Well . . . if you could help us actually *find* the place . . .

Tsukiko   A hundred yards further up the road . . . the first left . . . you won't miss it.

Tatsuo   Thank you so much!

Hiroshi   Oof, the old house – you're a braver man than I!

Tatsuo   What do you mean?

Tsukiko   If you need anything . . . anything at all . . . we're just next door. Call by any time.

Hiroshi   Welcome to the neighbourhood!

Hiroshi *and* **Tsukiko** *go to exit –* **Tsukiko** *gives* **Hiroshi** *a stern look.*

Hiroshi   What? What did I say?

Kanta *is left awkwardly staring at* **Satsuki**.

Satsuki   Hello.

Tsukiko   Kanta!

Kanta *nods a goodbye and runs away. The Ogakis have gone.*

Tatsuo   Shall we go and see our new home?

The girls cheer.

2 – The Old House

The Kusakabes arrive at their new home – a large wooden building, predominantly in the Japanese style, but with a two-storey European extension – it has definitely seen better days.

Behind the house is a large camphor tree. **Tatsuo** *and the* **Removal Man** *start unloading the truck.*

Tatsuo   This is it, girls!

Satsuki   Is this our house?

Tatsuo   I guess so.

Satsuki (*to* **Mei**)   Come on!

Satsuki *runs off to explore.*

Mei   Wait for me!

There's a water pump and a well. The girls have never had so much outside space – they run, they jump, they turn cartwheels and laugh deep from their bellies.

Satsuki *swings around a wooden support holding up an awning – the wood is rotten and the support moves dangerously.* **Mei** *and* **Satsuki** *both laugh.*

Satsuki *gives the support a kick.*

Mei *gives the support a good shake – the whole thing nearly comes tumbling down. A handful of acorns fall to the ground.*

Mei   What are they?

Satsuki   Acorns.

Tatsuo *is opening up the house.*

Tatsuo   What have you got there?

Satsuki   Acorns, I think. They fell from up there.

Tatsuo   It must be squirrels. (*Beat.*) So what do you think? First impressions.

Satsuki   The wood is rotten.

Tatsuo   It just needs a little care and attention.

Mei   There's so much space!

Tatsuo   We're not in Tokyo anymore, it's true. But the walk to school won't be much further than you're used to . . . with a few more trees maybe . . . fewer roads to cross. And we're that much closer to your . . . to the hospital.

Satsuki   It's perfect, Dad.

Tatsuo   You think?

Satsuki   Yes. Absolutely.

Mei   It's great!

The **Removal Man** *approaches, carrying a large radio cabinet.*

Tatsuo   Through here is fine. (*Handing keys to* **Satsuki**.) Why don't you go and open up?

Satsuki *and* **Mei** *head to the back of the house.*

3a – Haunted

Satsuki   Come on!

Mei   Wait for me!

They find the locked door to the kitchen. The house is ramshackle and a little bit frightening.

Satsuki   It's just an old house. (*Unlocks the door.*)

The door swings open, casting light into a pitch-black room. There is a darting and a rustling: **Soot-Sprites** *– small, round, black, furry things – cover every surface and disappear as soon as they are disturbed. They disappear into the floorboards, through cracks under doors and into the shadows.*

Mei   What was that?

Satsuki *gives her a look that tells her to be quiet.*

There is something in the middle of the floor – **Satsuki** *approaches and picks it up. An acorn. She sees another. And another. A trail leading further into the house.*

The acorns lead to a doorway. **Satsuki** *gently opens the door – a hidden staircase leading up to the attic floor.*

Satsuki   Hello? Is anybody there?

Mei   Come out, come out, wherever you are!

An acorn bounces down the staircase. Something is in the attic.
Satsuki *and* **Mei** *look up into the dark.*

Satsuki   It's no use hiding.

Mei   We know you're in there.

Deep breaths. Brave faces. The girls ascend the staircase.

3b – Haunted

The attic is dusty and full of cobwebs.

Satsuki *and* **Mei** *poke their heads through the access panel in the
floor and scream at the top of their lungs.*

Something moves. More **Soot-Sprites***! They scatter and hide.*

Satsuki *and* **Mei** *enter the loft space – it seems empty. The attic is
quiet. Then everything moves –* **Soot-Sprites** *everywhere.* **Satsuki**
runs back down the stairs, shouting as she goes.

Satsuki   Dad! Dad!

Mei *is alone in the attic. She waits, expecting something magical to
happen. A lone* **Soot-Sprite** *floats down in front of her. She claps
her hands together, capturing the little beast. An explosion of*
Soot-Sprites*!*

4 – Mei and the Soot-Sprites

Downstairs.

Tatsuo *is introducing* **Satsuki** *to* **Granny***.*

Tatsuo   Satsuki . . . I'd like you to meet . . . I'm sorry, what
should the children call you?

Granny   Please . . . call me Granny.

Tatsuo   This is Granny – she lives next door. This is Satsuki
– my eldest.

Granny   Hello, my dear.

Satsuki   Hello. It's nice to meet you.

Granny   And it's nice to meet you too.

Mei *enters – running at speed straight into* **Granny**.

Granny   Who's this little ball of energy?

Tatsuo   Mei! Oh gosh . . . I'm so sorry.

Mei *hides behind* **Satsuki**.

Tatsuo   Mei . . . this is Granny. She's been looking after the house.

Granny   I've tried to keep it clean as best as I can.

Tatsuo   Your face is filthy . . . and your hands . . . don't touch anything . . .

Mei   There were . . . there were . . . I thought they had gone . . . but they were just hiding . . . and then . . . and then . . . in the attic . . . hundreds of them . . . I caught one . . . I thought I had . . . in my hands . . . but . . . but . . .

Tatsuo   Slow down . . . what are you talking about?

Satsuki   I saw them too.

Tatsuo   What did you see?

Granny   Oh well . . . this is special . . . how wonderful. It seems you have soot-sprites living here.

Mei   Soot-sprites?

Granny   They move into old buildings that have been left empty for a time . . . they make a terrible mess . . . cover everything with dirt. My mother called them 'wandering soot'. And you both saw them, you say?

Tatsuo   What are they . . . some sort of ghost or goblin or . . .?

Granny   Don't worry . . . they won't cause you any trouble. If they like you, they'll simply move on without a word.

Tatsuo   I've always wanted to live in a haunted house.

Granny   Oh I wouldn't say it was *haunted*.

Mei   I don't want them to go anywhere.

Satsuki   What if there was a big one . . . the size of a beach ball . . . hiding in the dark . . . waiting for the moment to pounce . . . RAWRR!!

Tatsuo   Satsuki.

Mei   I'm not afraid. I'm not afraid of anything.

Tatsuo   That dress was clean on this morning.

Mei   Sorry, Daddy.

Tatsuo   And the floor . . . both of you . . . the state of your feet!

Satsuki   Sorry, Dad.

Granny   Come on, girls . . . why don't you help me clean up?

Tatsuo   You don't have to do that.

Granny   Nonsense. Do either of you know where the water pump is?

Granny *and the girls clean the house.*

Mei *and* **Satsuki** *pump water from the water pump.*

Tatsuo *opens the doors, shutters and windows of the house – letting the light in.*

Soot-Sprites *appear from the shadows and cause mischief.*

Song: 'Soot-Sprites'.

5 – The Little Boy Next Door

Satsuki *finds* **Kanta** *lurking by the water pump – looking curiously into the house. He has a basket in his hands.*

Satsuki   Hello again.

Kanta *doesn't answer.*

Satsuki   My name is Satsuki.

Kanta *doesn't answer.*

Satsuki   Your name is Kanta, isn't it?

Kanta   I . . . I . . .

Satsuki   We are going to be neighbours. Where is your house? Is it down the road? We used to be able to hear our old neighbours through the walls! The sky is so big here and the air is so clean. Are there bears in the woods? Or wild boar maybe? I've seen pigs before but never a wild boar. Are they scary? I saw some little fish in the stream. Do you think there might be frogspawn? Is there a pond nearby? Do you go to school in the village? Which class are you in? Is the teacher nice? Do you like gorillas? They have two at the zoo in Tokyo. I've seen them. (*Beats her chest like a gorilla.*) Can we walk to school together? (*The basket.*) Is that for us?

Kanta   My mum . . . she said . . . my mum said . . .

Satsuki   Yes?

Kanta   . . . to give this to Granny.

Satsuki   What is it?

Kanta (*under his breath*)   Take it . . . take it . . .

Satsuki   Excuse me?

Kanta   Take it!

Satsuki *takes the basket.*

Kanta *runs away.*

Granny (*looks up*)   Is that Kanta I can hear?

Satsuki   He brought us this basket.

Kanta (*from some distance away*)   YOUR HOUSE IS HAUNTED!

Granny   Kanta!

Kanta *exits as fast as he can.*

Granny   He's not usually quite so bad mannered. Let me take that . . . (*Takes the basket.*)

Tatsuo   What's all this?

Granny   A little care package . . . a light supper . . . a few odds and ends to get you settled.

Tatsuo   That's very considerate . . . thank you.

Mei   There's cake!

Satsuki   Let me see!

Granny   I'll let you settle in. We're just down the road should you need anything.

Mei   Goodbye, Granny!

Satsuki   Thank you.

Granny   Goodbye, girls! (*Exits.*)

Tatsuo   That was very kind of her. Where did we put the dishes?

Mei   I'll get them! (*Rushes off.*)

Satsuki *looks concerned.*

Tatsuo   Satsuki?

Satsuki   Why did that boy . . . why was he like that?

Tatsuo (*laughs*)   I was a little boy like him once.

Satsuki   Yuck.

6 – Evening Wind

Night is falling and the quiet of the countryside envelops the Kusakabe house.

Satsuki *is collecting wood from the wood store. It is dark and she is a little frightened. An owl hoots, startling* **Satsuki** *and causing her to trip and drop all of her wood.*

Tatsuo *appears from the house.*

Tatsuo   Satsuki . . .? We don't want the bathwater to get cold.

Satsuki   Just coming.

Tatsuo   What's wrong?

Satsuki   I tripped over. It's nothing.

Tatsuo (*takes the wood from her*)   It's dark out here, huh?

Satsuki   Yes.

Tatsuo   And quiet.

Satsuki   Yes.

Tatsuo   No streetlights or car horns or police sirens.

Satsuki   No.

Tatsuo   Not like our old place, is it?

Satsuki   No.

Tatsuo   Do you want to go back to our old place?

Satsuki   No . . .

Tatsuo   It's okay if you do. But we have to give this a try.

Satsuki   I know.

Tatsuo   Let's get this inside. We don't want the fire to go out.

Satsuki   Dad . . .?

Tatsuo   Yes?

Satsuki *looks up to the tree behind the house.*

Satsuki   What's that big tree?

Tatsuo   It is a camphor tree.

Satsuki   A camphor tree.

Tatsuo   It must be hundreds of years old . . . and it'll be here for hundreds more. It's magnificent, don't you think?

Mei *exits the house, brushing her teeth.*

Mei   This house is going to fall down.

Tatsuo   I hope not!

Mei   It's so old. It will probably fall down tonight.

Tatsuo   Then we better unpack our camping gear . . . just in case.

Wind in the trees. The hooting owl. The lights of the house flicker. The old building creaks and groans. The girls are scared.

Tatsuo *starts laughing – exaggeratedly, a little maniacally. His daughters look at him as though he's crazy.*

Tatsuo   Come on . . . laugh with me. (*Laughs.*)

Mei *laughs.*

Tatsuo   We should all laugh.

Satsuki *tries to laugh.*

Tatsuo   It's impossible to be scared when you're laughing. (*Laughs.*)

Mei *laughs.*

Satsuki *laughs.*

Tatsuo   Laugh at the owl . . . laugh at the moon . . . laugh at the big spooky trees!

They are all laughing, and things don't seem so frightening anymore.

Tatsuo   There we go. Anyone still scared?

Satsuki   No.

Tatsuo   Good.

Mei   I wasn't scared in the first place.

Satsuki   Liar.

Mei   I wasn't!

Tatsuo   Let's go inside.

Mei *and* **Tatsuo** *head inside, but* **Satsuki** *needs to be brave for herself. She steps forward into the dark of the night.*

The **Soot-Sprites** *emerge from the nooks and crannies of the house – they swirl in the air like a flock of starlings.*

Satsuki *sees them and, instead of feeling scared, she chooses to laugh. The* **Soot-Sprites** *swirl around* **Satsuki**. *The laughter is genuine now. The* **Soot-Sprites** *lift off and disappear into the night sky.* **Satsuki** *waves them goodbye.*

7 – Let's Go to the Hospital

Morning. The local rice fields.

The Ogakis – **Hiroshi**, **Tsukiko**, **Kanta** *and* **Granny** *– along with a few other* **Workers** *from the village, are planting rice plants.*

The Kusakabes – **Tatsuo**, **Satsuki** *and* **Mei** *– enter. They are all perched on* **Tatsuo**'s *bicycle.*

Granny   Hello there, Kusakabes!

Tatsuo   Good morning!

Hiroshi   Where are you Kusakabes off to?

Mei   We're going to see Mummy.

Satsuki   She's in the hospital.

Hiroshi   Oh . . . I'm sorry to hear that . . .

Satsuki   It is why we moved here.

Hiroshi   Is she very sick?

Very awkward silence.

Tatsuo   She is getting better. And the country air is doing her good. Say goodbye, girls.

Mei   Goodbye!

Satsuki   Goodbye.

Tatsuo *starts pedalling and the Kusakabes exit on their bicycle.*

Granny   Those poor girls.

Kanta   What's wrong with their mother?

8 – Mother

Shichikokuyama Tuberculosis Hospital.

Tatsuo   We're here to see my wife – Yasuko Kusakabe.

Nurse   Of course, Mr Kusakabe. Though the doctor would like to speak to you first, if that's alright?

Tatsuo   I have my children . . .

Nurse   I'll take them through. My colleague will take you to the doctor. This way, children.

*The nurse (**Nurse Emiko**) leads **Mei** and **Satsuki** to their mother's ward.*

Nurse   My name is Nurse Emiko.

Mei   Thank you for looking after our mummy, Nurse Emiko.

Satsuki   Thank you, Nurse Emiko.

Nurse   And you must be Mei?

Mei   Yes.

Nurse   And so you would be Satsuki?

Satsuki   That's right.

Nurse   Your mother has spoken a lot about both of you.

Mei   Can she come home soon?

Nurse   That's not for me to decide.

Mei   Who does decide?

Nurse   Well . . . that's a conversation between your parents and the doctor.

Yasuko Kusakabe *is sat up in bed*.

Nurse   Mrs Kusakabe . . . you have some visitors.

The girls run and hug their mother.

Yasuko   My girls . . . oh I've missed you.

Mei   Daddy didn't know the way and we took a wrong turning and we ended up in a field and I got mud on my shoes and there was a cow –

Yasuko   You're here now. That's what matters. Hello, Satsuki.

Satsuki   Hello.

Yasuko   Where is your father?

Satsuki   Taking to the doctor.

Mei   When are you coming home?

Yasuko   I think they want to take care of me here for a little longer.

Mei   We can take care of you at home.

Satsuki   These are *doctors* and *nurses*, Mei. We can't care for Mum like they can.

Mei   We can try.

Yasuko   Tell me about the new house – are you settling in?

Satsuki   Yes, thank you. The neighbours are very nice . . . and there is a stream . . . and a really big tree . . . and . . . (*quietly*) . . . the house is haunted.

Mei   Satsuki!

Satsuki   Mei is worried you might not come home if you know that the house is haunted.

Yasuko   That all depends on the ghosts, doesn't it?

Mei   Soot-Sprites.

Satsuki   I think it is better that you know so that you can be prepared.

Yasuko   Are they scary, Mei?

Mei   No.

Satsuki   I think they've gone now anyway.

Yasuko   I like your hair – did your father cut it?

Satsuki   Yes.

Yasuko   He's done a good job. Do you like it this short? (*Pulls* **Satsuki** *close and starts brushing her hair.*) My hair was exactly the same at your age.

Satsuki   Was it?

Yasuko   It was.

Satsuki   I do like it like this.

Mei   Brush my hair!

Satsuki   Wait your turn. (*Beat.*) Do you think it'll look like yours when I grow up?

Yasuko   Maybe.

Satsuki   I hope so.

Tatsuo *enters with* **Nurse Emiko**.

Tatsuo   Satsuki – take your sister outside.

Mei   Mummy was going to brush my hair.

Tatsuo   Later.

Mei   I don't want to go.

Nurse   I think there's some ice cream in the kitchen . . .

Mei   I want to stay with Mummy.

Yasuko   Go on . . . it's okay.

Satsuki   Come on, Mei.

Mei   No.

Yasuko   I would quite like some ice cream. Will you bring me back some?

Mei   Okay.

Mei *squeezes* **Yasuko** *tightly.*

Yasuko   Off you go.

Mei, **Satsuki** *and* **Nurse Emiko** *exit.* **Tatsuo** *and* **Yasuko** *are alone.*

Yasuko   Hello.

Tatsuo   Hello.

Yasuko   You've spoken to the doctor?

Tatsuo   Yes.

Tatsuo *sits on the bed. They hug each other. They hold each other in silence for a long time.*

Song: 'Mother'.

9a – A Little Creature

Morning – the Kusakabe house.

Satsuki *opens the screen doors to let light into the house. She is simultaneously cooking breakfast and preparing lunchboxes. She is dressed and ready for school. She chops vegetables and cooks rice.* **Mei** *is helping.*

Satsuki (*calls off*)   Dad!

Tatsuo *enters, rubbing the sleep from his eyes.*

Tatsuo   What's all this?

Mei   Breakfast.

Satsuki   And lunch.

Tatsuo   Oh . . . Satsuki . . . school! I completely forgot. I should be doing that.

Satsuki   You sit down and eat your breakfast. You too, Mei.

Tatsuo *and* **Mei** *sit down to eat.* **Satsuki** *serves them breakfast. They all eat.*

Tatsuo   It's good. Thank you.

A voice in the distance.

Voice (*off*)   Satsuki!

Satsuki (*replies*)   Coming!

Tatsuo   Who's that?

Satsuki   A girl in my class. We're walking to school together.

Tatsuo   Already making friends?

Satsuki   I have to go. (*Gathers her school things.*) Bye, Dad. Bye, Mei!

Tatsuo   Have a good day!

Satsuki *exits. The house is suddenly very quiet.* **Tatsuo** *looks at* **Mei**. **Mei** *looks at* **Tatsuo**.

Tatsuo   I guess it's just you and me.

Mei   I have errands to run.

Tatsuo   Oh.

9b – A Little Creature

Tatsuo *sits in his office – the doors open onto the veranda. He sits, surrounded by books, writing copious notes.*

Mei *plays in front of the house. She is picking flowers. She finds something on the ground – a small piece of ceramic. She brushes the dirt off and inspects it. She takes her piece of treasure and her flowers over to her father.*

Tatsuo (*the flowers*)   Those are very beautiful.

Mei   You be the flower shop, Daddy.

Tatsuo   Am I a florist now?

Mei   Yes.

Tatsuo   Who am I to sell them to?

Mei   To whoever comes by.

Tatsuo   What if no one comes by?

Mei   You won't get very far with that attitude. (*Beat.*) I found something. (*Gives the piece of ceramic to **Tatsuo**.*)

Tatsuo (*inspecting the broken piece of pot*)   Oh . . . wow . . . this is very interesting . . . very interesting indeed . . .

Mei   It's a piece of broken pot.

Tatsuo   I can see that.

Mei   How old is it?

Tatsuo   Quite old, I should think.

Mei   Don't you know?

Tatsuo   How is a florist meant to assess the age of broken pots?

Mei   You're not a florist now – you're Daddy.

Tatsuo   In that case . . . let me see . . . oh yes . . . very old . . .

Mei   A hundred years old?

Tatsuo   Maybe even older.

Mei   Really?

Tatsuo   Can you find the rest of it, do you think?

Mei   I'll go and look.

Tatsuo   Stay where I can see you.

Mei *stomps off looking for more pieces of pot.* **Tatsuo** *returns to his work.*

9c – A Little Creature

Mei *is searching for more pieces of pot. She doesn't find any. What she does find is an acorn. She picks it up and looks at it.*

She puts it in her little bag. She looks around. Another acorn. She puts that in her bag as well. She looks around – more acorns. She puts all the acorns she finds in her little bag.

Out of the grass comes **Shōtotoro**. *He keeps his distance from* **Mei** *but watches her closely. As* **Mei** *collects acorns,* **Shōtotoro** *follows – trying to get closer to the stash of acorns in* **Mei**'s *bag.*

Mei *senses she is being followed. She turns swiftly and catches* **Shōtotoro** *behind her.* **Shōtotoro** *freezes.* **Mei** *takes a step towards* **Shōtotoro**. **Shōtotoro** *takes a step back.*

Mei   I'm not going to hurt you.

Shōtotoro *freaks out and makes a dash for it.*

Mei   Come back!

Shōtotoro *jumps into a metal bucket and disappears out of sight.*

Mei *creeps up to the bucket, not wanting to spook the creature. She reaches the bucket and picks it up in triumph. But the bucket is empty. The bottom of the bucket has rusted out completely and* **Mei** *holds it up to look all the way through.*

Shōtotoro *appears some distance from* **Mei**.

Mei *sees him through the bottom of the bucket.*

Mei   Hey!

Shōtotoro *runs away as* **Mei** *chases him. He disappears into an opening beneath the house.* **Mei** *runs up to the opening and tries to look inside – she takes off her bag to do so. She gets on her hands and knees and sticks her head underneath the house.*

Shōtotoro *and* **Chōtotoro** *peer around the corner of the house.*

Chōtotoro *starts to sneak away – not wanting to be detected by* **Mei**. **Shōtotoro** *stops* **Chōtotoro** *and indicates* **Mei**'*s bag.*

Mei *still has her head beneath the house, looking for* **Shōtotoro**.

Chōtotoro *sneaks up to* **Mei**'*s bag and takes a look inside. He looks back at* **Shōtotoro**, *at* **Mei** *and then back to the bag. Look at all those acorns!* **Chōtotoro** *grabs the bag and runs.* **Shōtotoro** *follows.*

Mei *turns to discover what's happening.*

Mei   Hey! HEY! That's mine!

Mei *chases* **Shōtotoro** *and* **Chōtotoro** *as they disappear into the woods surrounding the house.*

10a – Totoro

Mei *chases the two totoro through the thick tangle of the forest.* **Mei**'*s clothes get caught on branches, her hat gets knocked off and left behind.*

Chōtotoro *and* **Shōtotoro** *are faster than their little legs would suggest. They run further into the dark and ancient forest.* **Mei** *manages to keep them in sight. She clambers over tree roots and rocks.*

She clambers up an incline and into a clearing. She has lost sight of the two totoro.

At the centre of the clearing stands the old camphor tree – massive and ancient. Tied around the trunk of the tree is a large rope. A small shrine to one side of the tree.

Mei *looks up at the huge, magical tree.*

From the tangled roots of the tree watch the two totoro. **Mei** *catches sight of them and they disappear into a burrow at the base of the tree.*

Mei *puffs up her chest and clambers over the roots to the opening of the burrow. She sticks her head in. She calls out.*

Mei   Hello?

Her voice echoes.

She leans further in, but she loses her footing and tumbles into the burrow.

10b – Totoro

Mei *is falling through the roots of the ancient tree.*

She lands with a dizzying bump.

Dazed, **Mei** *looks around, wondering where she is. She finds herself in a dark, hollowed-out cavity beneath the camphor tree. It is dark and little bit frightening. Toadstools and bracket fungi. Damp moss and ferns.*

Mei *picks herself up and brushes herself down. Light filters in from somewhere above, but she cannot see a way out.*

She explores her new surroundings. She is starting to get a little frightened.

Mei *is not alone.*

Sleeping in the tree hollow is a large creature. As it breathes, its ribcage rises and falls. The creature's breath is heavy and slow – a deep, rumbling sound.

Mei *approaches the sleeping giant.*

This is **Ōtotoro** *– the largest and oldest of the three totoro.*

Mei *gently approaches.* **Ōtotoro** *shifts in his sleep and* **Mei** *jumps back. But her curiosity outweighs her nervousness. She steps forward once again, hand outstretched. She touches* **Ōtotoro**'s *bulbous tail.*

Ōtotoro *flicks his tail, swatting away* **Mei***'s hand as though she were a fly.*

Mei *will not be discouraged. She reaches out once again and starts stroking* **Ōtotoro***'s fur.*

Mei   My name is Mei . . . I'm four years old. It's nice to meet you. We've just moved in next door . . . we're neighbours. Would you like a toffee?

Ōtotoro *flicks his tail and bats* **Mei** *square in the face, knocking her to the floor.*

Mei *leaps straight back – very up for a spot of play-fighting. She squares off against* **Ōtotoro***'s tail and leaps at it – grabbing on with both hands.*

Ōtotoro *rolls over –* **Mei** *disappears from view.* **Ōtotoro** *scratches his belly, yawns and falls straight back to sleep.*

Mei *appears from behind* **Ōtotoro** *– climbing his belly like a mountain. She positions herself on his stomach.*

Ōtotoro *opens his eyes and curiously, but lethargically, inspects the tiny human that now sits on him.*

Ōtotoro *yawns.* **Mei** *reaches out and rubs* **Ōtotoro***'s nose.*

Mei*'s tickling makes* **Ōtotoro** *sneeze – it's incredibly loud!* **Mei** *is knocked from her perch and disappears once more.*

Again she climbs back to the top of **Ōtotoro***'s belly. She brushes herself down. She pokes at* **Ōtotoro***'s face until he opens his eyes.*

Mei   What's your name?

Ōtotoro   *Doh-doh-ohhh.*

Mei   'Toh-toh-roe'? Is that your name?

Ōtotoro   *Doh-doh-ohhh.*

Mei   Totoro.

Ōtotoro *grumbles and closes his eyes.* **Mei** *prods him until his eyes open. He opens his mouth wide – so wide he could easily eat* **Mei** *in one bite – and roars. He roars so loudly that the entire tree shakes.*

Mei *is not intimidated. She takes a deep breath and lets out her own roar.*

Ōtotoro *roars in return.*

Mei *roars.*

A roaring contest.

Ōtotoro *can't seem to frighten this little girl.*

Ōtotoro   *Doh-doh-ohhh.*

He settles back down to sleep. **Mei** *climbs back to the top of* **Ōtotoro***'s belly and nuzzles down.*

Mei   We're friends now, Totoro.

Ōtotoro *closes his eyes and goes back to sleep.* **Mei** *rests on his belly and falls asleep.*

Chōtotoro *and* **Shōtotoro** *appear from behind the roots. They look at each other – they don't know what to make of this strange little human interloper. They open* **Mei***'s little yellow bag and start eating her lunch.*

11 – Home from School

Tatsuo *is still at work in his study.*

Satsuki *arrives home from school.*

Voice (*off*)   See you tomorrow, Satsuki!

Satsuki   Goodbye! (*Calls out.*) Dad! Mei! I'm home!

Tatsuo   Is it that time already? How was school?

Satsuki   Okay, thank you.

Tatsuo   How are you getting on with your teacher?

Satsuki   We're looking at things I've already studied so I'm helping her with the younger children.

Tatsuo   You're there to learn, Satsuki . . . not to teach. What books are you reading at the moment?

Satsuki *opens her bag and shows him.*

Tatsuo (*approves*)   If you need me to bring you anything from Tokyo . . . the university library has . . .

Satsuki   I have everything I need.

Tatsuo   Are you making friends?

Satsuki   I am. Where's Mei?

Tatsuo   She was just playing outside. Mei?! I told her not to wander off.

Satsuki   I'll go and look for her.

Tatsuo   Let me just put some shoes on.

Satsuki *looks for* **Mei**.

Satsuki   Mei! I'm back from school! Mei?!

Satsuki *finds* **Mei***'s hat at the edge of the forest. She picks it up.*

Satsuki   Mei.

12 – The Huge Tree in the Tsukamori Forest

At the base of the camphor tree.

Mei *is fast asleep on a pile of leaves.*

The voices of **Satsuki** *and* **Tatsuo** *in the distance.*

Tatsuo (*off*)   Mei!

Satsuki (*off*)   Come out, come out, wherever you are!

Mei (*gently waking up*)   Totoro . . .?

Mei *looks around – she sees that her bag has been returned to her.*

Satsuki *enters with* **Tatsuo** *following behind – he is wearing* **Mei**'s *hat.*

Satsuki   There you are. You need to stay near the house. What were you thinking?

Mei   Where has he gone?

Satsuki   Who?

Mei   He was big and furry . . . with whiskers and pointy little ears . . . a large mouth and claws . . . teeth . . . he roared and shouted but I wasn't scared.

Satsuki   You were dreaming.

Mei   I didn't dream it . . . I didn't make him up!

Tatsuo   Who's this now?

Satsuki   Mei saw a bear.

Tatsuo   A bear?!

Mei   I know what a bear looks like.

Tatsuo   There are no bears around here.

Mei   He lives under this tree . . . I climbed through a hole . . . I'll show you . . .

Mei *can't find the entrance.*

Mei   He was big and round and I fell asleep on his belly. And I know what a bear looks like. I'm not lying.

Tatsuo   No one thinks you're lying.

Mei   Satsuki does.

Satsuki   I don't . . . but maybe you just . . . maybe you were just pretending and . . .

Mei   I think the little ones ate my lunch.

Tatsuo   It sounds like you've met one of the spirits of the forest, which makes you a very lucky girl. A long time ago . . . when the land was covered in trees . . . man lived alongside the animals, and the spirits of the land and the sea lived with us . . . they protected us and the forest gave us all we needed . . . but as man grew, he chopped down the trees to build houses . . . to build cities . . . we made animals our pets . . . our food . . . our labour . . . and the spirits of the forest started to hide from us . . . frightened but also disappointed. Now they don't show themselves at all . . . and certainly not to grown-ups like me. But once in a while they meet someone . . . someone like you Mei . . . and they like you . . . and so they let you see them . . . so you know that they are there . . . protecting you.

Mei   Will I see them again?

Tatsuo   That's up to them.

Satsuki   Will I see them, Dad?

Tatsuo   That's up to them also. (*Looks up at the tree.*) It really is a magnificent tree. When I first saw it . . . when I was looking for somewhere for us to live . . . I knew that this was a good place . . . somewhere we could call home . . . for you girls . . . for your mother . . . give her something to look forward to. (*Calls up to the tree.*) Spirit of the forest . . . thank you for watching over Mei . . . thank you for making us feel so welcome in our new home . . . please watch over Mei and Satsuki . . . please watch over their mother, Yasuko . . . please continue to watch over us all. (*Beat.*) Last one home is a rotten egg!

Tatsuo *dashes off.*

Satsuki (*following him*)   Hey! No fair!

Mei   Wait up! (*To the tree.*) See you soon, Totoro. (*Runs off after her sister and father.*)

13 – Kanta and his Chickens

The yard of the Ogakis' house.

Kanta *is feeding the chickens.*

Kanta   Hey chickens . . . breakfast time for you . . . how many eggs are you going to lay today, do you think?

The chickens cluck.

Kanta   That many, huh? Be careful not to do yourself an injury.

The chickens cluck.

Kanta   No, I can't . . . I have school today.

The chickens cluck.

Kanta   Yeah . . . it's boring . . . I don't see the point.

The chickens cluck.

Kanta   Nobody asked you.

Satsuki *and* **Mei** *arrive at the house and are greeted by* **Tsukiko** *and* **Granny**.

The chickens cluck.

Kanta   Them? They're our new neighbours.

The chickens cluck.

Kanta   No, I don't like the look of them either.

Satsuki *waves at* **Kanta** *and starts walking over.*

Kanta   Look out, she's coming over. (*Throws more feed to the chickens.*)

Satsuki   Hello.

Kanta *doesn't respond.*

Satsuki   My dad is working at the university today . . . in Tokyo . . . he's giving a lecture on 'Palaeolithic burial offerings'. So Granny's looking after Mei while I'm at school. (*Beat.*) Are these your chickens?

Kanta   Yes.

Satsuki   I can wait for you to finish if you would like to walk to school together? Will you be long?

Kanta *doesn't respond.*

Satsuki   Okay . . . well . . . I'll see you in class then. Goodbye, chickens.

Satsuki *exits. The chickens cluck.*

Kanta   I don't know what you're talking about.

The chickens cluck.

Kanta   She's not my girlfriend!

The chickens cluck.

Kanta   Shut up, chickens.

14 – Granny and Mei

Mei *is helping* **Granny** *with the laundry.* **Mei** *is stamping on the wet laundry in a tub.* **Granny** *is scrubbing.*

Granny   What do you and your sister do to get your clothes so filthy?

Mei   We just play.

Granny   And what do you play?

Mei *shrugs.*

Granny   Nice to have a sister.

Mei   I guess.

Granny   Someone to go on adventures with.

Mei   I can have adventures by myself.

Granny   And what sort of adventures do you go on 'by yourself'?

Mei   Oh . . . you know . . . (*Beat.*) Do you have a sister?

Granny I did.

Mei Where is she now?

Granny I want to hear about your adventures.

Mei (*whispers*) I met Totoro!

Granny 'Totoro'?

Mei Do you know him?

Granny I can't say that I do.

Mei He's big and he smells like mud and lets out a roar like this: (*Roars.*)

Granny He sounds scary.

Mei He's my friend. Daddy says he's the 'spirit of the forest'.

Granny That's enough now. Help me to hang it up.

Granny and **Mei** *hang out the laundry.*

Mei Is your sister dead?

Granny *stops and looks at* **Mei**. *She knows this is a delicate subject.*

Granny Yes she is.

Mei How did she die?

Granny It was a long time ago.

Mei Do you miss her?

Granny I do.

Mei I'm sorry.

Granny That's okay. (*Beat.*) If your friend really is a forest spirit, he could be very old indeed.

Mei Do you think so?

Granny He could be hundreds of years old . . . thousands even!

Mei   As old as you?

Granny (*laughs*)   Maybe . . . maybe.

Silence.

Mei   My mummy is very sick.

Granny   I know, dear.

Mei   She's getting better though.

Granny   That's good to hear. (*Beat.*) Stay here . . . I have something I want to show you. (*Exits.*)

Mei *is alone. It is quiet. There is a cold breeze.*

Granny *re-enters carrying a model aircraft.*

Granny   Here . . . this is Kanta's . . . do you like it?

Mei   I guess.

Granny   I'm sure he won't mind if you play with it . . . as long as you're careful.

Granny *continues to hang the laundry.* **Mei** *gets quickly bored with the model plane. She stands up.*

Mei   Okay, Granny . . . I'm going now.

Granny   Oh are you? Can I ask where it is that you're going?

Mei   To the forest.

Granny   To see your friend?

Mei   Totoro.

Granny   I am afraid you need to stay here with me.

Mei   I'm going to see Totoro.

Granny   I can't be traipsing through the woods at my age.

Mei   I can go on my own.

Granny   Come and sit down . . . be a good girl.

Mei   No.

Granny   When I speak with your father . . . he will ask if you were well-behaved. What would you like me to tell him?

Mei   That I've gone to see Totoro.

Granny   Mei, please do as you are told.

Mei *sits down near* **Granny**. *She takes the model plane and plays with it for a bit. She throws it into the air. The plane crashes into the ground and breaks into pieces.*

Granny   Mei!

15 – Satsuki at School

Classroom.

It is break-time and **Satsuki** *is helping* **Miss Hara**, *her teacher, ready the room for the afternoon class.*

Miss Hara   You don't need to do that, Satsuki. Go outside and play with your friends.

Satsuki   It's no trouble. I like to be helpful.

Miss Hara   Well, it's very much appreciated. (*Beat.*) How are you settling in?

Satsuki   Very well, thank you Miss Hara.

Miss Hara   It takes a little while sometimes . . . new surroundings . . . new people . . .

Satsuki   Everyone has been incredibly welcoming.

Miss Hara   Oh good. (*Beat.*) You lived in Tokyo before you moved here?

Satsuki   Yes.

Miss Hara   It must have been busy . . . the big city . . . electric light in the street . . . a telephone in every house . . .

Satsuki My next-door neighbour had a television.

Miss Hara Really? It'll be some time before we see a television around here, I'm afraid.

Satsuki I don't mind. I've seen all kinds of flowers and trees that I haven't seen before. And there are creatures in the woods . . . I've not seen them . . . my sister has.

Miss Hara Oh yes . . . foxes and monkeys and deer . . . all kinds. My grandfather told me there were wolves in these forests when he was young.

Satsuki Wolves?

Miss Hara Not anymore. Not around here. When you move to a new place things can seem frightening . . . but you'll see . . . there are no monsters in the woods.

Satsuki I would like to have seen a wolf.

Granny *enters, leading* **Mei** *by the hand.* **Mei** *is visibly upset.*

Satsuki Mei!

Miss Hara Mrs Ogaki . . . is everything alright?

Granny Yes . . . well . . . I . . .

Satsuki Mei? What's wrong?

Mei, *shy, doesn't respond.*

Miss Hara Is this your sister?

Satsuki Yes, Miss Hara.

Miss Hara It's nice to meet you, Mei.

Mei *doesn't respond.*

Granny I'm sorry . . . I tried . . . but she wouldn't stop crying . . . she kept trying to run to the forest. I didn't know what else to do.

Mei *is crying.*

Satsuki   Hey . . . don't . . . don't cry . . . (*Beat.*) Miss Hara
. . . can Mei sit with me this afternoon . . . in class? That's
alright, isn't it? She won't be any trouble.

Miss Hara   Are you happy to do that, Mei? You'll sit quietly
. . . won't you?

Mei *mumbles.*

Satsuki   'Yes, Miss Hara.'

Mei   Yes, Miss Hara.

Miss Hara   Okay then.

Satsuki   Thank you.

The school bell rings. Break-time is over.

Miss Hara   Take your seats, girls.

Granny   Thank you.

16 – The Walk Home

*The road from the school to the Kusakabe house. A wayside shrine
– a Jizō statue.*

A rumble of thunder. It starts to rain.

Satsuki and **Mei** *run through the rain, looking for cover.* **Satsuki**
holds her schoolbag over her head to keep herself dry. **Mei** *tries to
hang onto her hat and clings to a crayon drawing of* **Ōtotoro**.

Satsuki   This way!

Mei *trips over as she runs and falls flat on her face.*

Satsuki *stops, runs to her, and helps her up.*

Mei (*holding up her drawing*)   My picture got wet. I wanted to
give it to Mummy.

Satsuki   When we get home I'll help you to draw another
one. You can even use my crayons.

Mei   Okay.

The girls shelter under the roof of the shrine.

Satsuki (*bowing to the statue*)   Excuse me, sir . . . but it's raining and we don't have an umbrella. I hope you don't mind if we share your roof for a while?

Mei (*bowing*)   We will be very well-behaved.

Kanta *enters. He holds his umbrella above his head – it is tatty and is full of holes. He sees* **Satsuki** *and* **Mei** *at the shrine and puts his head down as he walks past.*

Satsuki *has tried too many times to engage* **Kanta** *in conversation and she's too sad to try again, she just looks at the ground.*

Kanta *stops some distance beyond the shrine. He turns around and walks back. He stands in front of* **Satsuki** *and offers her his umbrella.*

Satsuki   But don't *you* need this?

Kanta *presses the umbrella into her hand and runs away.* **Satsuki** *and* **Mei** *watch as* **Kanta** *runs off through the rain.*

Mei   He's very odd.

Satsuki (*holds up the umbrella*)   Shall we go home?

Mei   This umbrella is full of holes.

17 – Kanta's Umbrella

The Ogakis' house.

Kanta, *stripped down to his pants and vest, is trying to get dry.*

Tsukiko *is hanging out his sodden clothes.*

Tsukiko   Honestly, Kanta . . .

Kanta   I just left it behind.

Tsukiko   Who else could leave their umbrella at school during a rainstorm?!

Granny *enters – she is holding the broken model aircraft. She hands it to* **Kanta**.

Granny   I can't have been looking where I was going.

Tsukiko   It's his own fault for leaving it lying around.

Granny   No, no . . . I'm just getting clumsy in my old age. I'll get you some glue. (*Exits.*)

Kanta *inspects his broken toy.*

Tsukiko   What are we going to do with you, eh Kanta?

Satsuki *and* **Mei** *appear at the door – dressed in wellies and raincoats and holding umbrellas.*

Satsuki   Is anybody home?

Kanta, *embarrassed to be seen in his underwear, runs away.*

Tsukiko   Oh Satsuki . . . Mei . . . come in . . . come in . . .

Satsuki   Thank you, but we're on our way to meet Dad – he forgot his umbrella this morning.

Tsukiko   That reminds me of someone else I know.

Satsuki   I wanted to return Kanta's umbrella. He lent it to us on the way home. It was really very kind of him.

Tsukiko (*takes the umbrella*)   Oh gosh . . . look at the state of this thing!

Satsuki   It kept us dry though . . . so thank him for me?

Tsukiko   He lent you this?

Satsuki   He did.

Tsukiko   Well I never.

Satsuki   Our dad's bus is due in a couple of minutes.

Tsukiko   Off you go, girls. Try to keep dry.

Satsuki   We will do.

Mei   Goodbye.

Satsuki *and* **Mei** *exit.* **Tsukiko** *sees* **Kanta** *hiding in the doorway, watching and listening. She ruffles his hair as she passes.*

Tsukiko   You're a funny fish, Kanta Ogaki. A funny little fish.

18a – A Soaking Wet Monster

A bus stop on a quiet country road. A streetlight.

Satsuki *and* **Mei** *are waiting in the rain beneath* **Satsuki***'s red umbrella. Their father's larger, black, more business-looking umbrella hangs from a sign on the bus stop.*

A bus arrives. A couple of people get off, but there's no sign of their father.

Bus Driver   Are you girls getting on?

Satsuki *shakes her head.*

Bus Driver   Okay.

The doors close and the bus pulls away.

Mei   He wasn't on the bus.

Satsuki   No.

Mei   Where is he?

Satsuki   He must have missed his connection.

Mei   Oh.

Satsuki   He'll be on the next one.

Mei   Okay.

The girls are alone. It's starting to get dark.

18b – A Soaking Wet Monster

It's quite dark now. The streetlight flickers on.

Mei   I'm tired.

Satsuki   It won't be long now. Look!

A light in the distance, heading their way.

It's not the bus. It's a woman in a rain-poncho on a bicycle. She cycles by.

Mei *sighs audibly.*

Satsuki *is starting to get worried.*

Satsuki   The bus is late, isn't it?

Mei   Uh-huh.

Satsuki   He'll be here soon. Here.

Satsuki *squats down and* **Mei** *climbs onto her back.*

18c – A Soaking Wet Monster

It's very dark now, and quite frightening.

Satsuki *doesn't know what to do.* **Mei** *has fallen asleep on* **Satsuki***'s back.*

The streetlight flickers – a dodgy wire somewhere inside.

Satsuki   Where are you, Dad? Come on . . . please . . .

A thump in the darkness.

Satsuki *is nervous.*

Another thump.

Out of the black of the surrounding woodland walks **Ōtotoro***. Thump, thump, thump as he walks. He stands at the bus stop next to* **Satsuki***. He wears a leaf on his head to keep off the rain – it is not very effective.*

Satsuki *is scared stiff.*

The rain comes down.

Satsuki *cannot get a clear view of the monster because of her red umbrella – he seems to just be waiting for a bus.* **Mei** *is fast asleep.* **Satsuki** *tries to sneak a look.*

Ōtotoro *scratches himself.*

They stand there together at the bus stop for a moment.

Satsuki   Are you . . . are you Totoro?

Ōtotoro *looks at* **Satsuki** *in acknowledgement.*

Satsuki (*tentatively smiles*)   Are you not getting rained on?

Ōtotoro *sniffs.*

Satsuki *takes her father's umbrella from the bus stop and offers it to the monster.*

Satsuki   Here . . . take it.

Ōtotoro *looks at the umbrella – not entirely sure what he's meant to do with it.*

Satsuki   You open it like this . . . see?

Satsuki *opens the umbrella, the action of which startles* **Ōtotoro**.

Satsuki   Don't be frightened . . . it's just an umbrella . . . like mine.

She offers it to him again. **Ōtotoro** *takes it. He turns it over, he sniffs it.*

Satsuki   Like this. (*Models her umbrella.*)

Ōtotoro *mimics* **Satsuki** *– holds the umbrella aloft.*

Satsuki   There you go. It'll keep you dry.

Ōtotoro *smiles in gratitude.*

Satsuki   You're welcome.

Ōtotoro *is amused by the sound of the rain on the umbrella.*

Satsuki   It makes a good noise, doesn't it . . . the rain?
'*Pitter-patter . . . pitter-patter . . .*'

Ōtotoro *jumps high into the air. His heavy landing causes all the branches of the trees to shed any rainwater and it all comes down in a massive rush. This makes* **Ōtotoro** *laugh very loudly.*

Mei *wakes up.*

Mei   Totoro . . .?

Satsuki   I can see him, Mei . . . I can see him!

There are headlights in the distance.

Something is not quite right – the beams from the headlights dart around. There is a low rumbling, but not of an engine, of many large, padded feet running at speed.

Into sight comes the **Catbus**. *As much of a cat as it is a bus, the* **Catbus**' *eyes are also its headlights, it propels itself forward on twelve legs, it's the size of a school bus and with enough room inside to carry two dozen passengers. A destination plate reads: 'FOREST'. Its large head swings around as it sniffs at* **Mei** *and* **Satsuki**.

Mei *and* **Satsuki** *are dumbstruck! The* **Catbus** *meows.*

Ōtotoro *makes his way to the door of the* **Catbus**. *He turns and hands a small parcel, neatly wrapped in a dried leaf, to* **Mei**. *He climbs aboard the* **Catbus** *– the umbrella still in his hand.*

The **Catbus** *purrs before bounding off down the road.*

Mei   Goodbye, Totoro!

Satsuki   Safe journey home!

The **Catbus** *and* **Ōtotoro** *have gone.*

Satsuki   Totoro . . . he . . . did he just steal Dad's umbrella?

Mei *and* **Satsuki** *are alone at the bus stop once again. They look off in the direction of the* **Catbus** *and hardly notice when their father's bus arrives at the stop.*

The door of the bus opens and **Tatsuo** *steps out.*

Tatsuo   Hello, girls!

The two girls hug their father tightly.

Tatsuo   I'm sorry I was late . . . I had a meeting that overran . . . and then my train was delayed . . . and I had to wait for the next bus . . . were you worried?

Satsuki   We met Totoro!

Mei   Totoro!

Satsuki *and* **Tatsuo** *start walking.*

Mei *holds in her hands the little parcel – a magical object.* **Mei** *stares at it, waiting for it to reveal its magic.*

Tatsuo   Mei!

Mei *runs off to join her father and sister. The three of them walk home hand-in-hand, jumping in puddles along the way.*

Song: 'My Neighbour Totoro'.

19a – Satsuki's Letter

Shichikokuyama Tuberculosis Hospital.

Yasuko *is sat by a window, reading a book.*

Nurse Emiko *enters with a letter.*

Nurse   How are you feeling this morning?

Yasuko   A little tired.

Nurse *places the back of her hand on* **Yasuko**'s *forehead.*

Yasuko   I don't think I have a fever.

Nurse   I just like to check. Are you coughing?

Yasuko   Less and less.

Nurse   If you feel any worse, let me or one of the other nurses know.

Yasuko   I'm just not sleeping very well.

Nurse   Better safe than sorry. (*Beat.*) I have something that will cheer you up. (*Hands her the letter.*)

Yasuko   A letter?

Nurse   From your daughters, I expect.

Yasuko   Satsuki's handwriting.

Nurse   I'll leave you to it.

Yasuko   Stay? I could use the company.

Nurse   Sure.

Yasuko *reads.*

19b – Satsuki's Letter

Satsuki *narrates her letter.*

Satsuki (*letter*)   Dear Mum. I hope you are feeling better. I am settling well into school and Miss Hara, my teacher, is very pleased with my work. We are playing lots outside and I am making plenty of new friends . . . though the little boy who lives next door is very annoying. Mei has met a forest spirit called Totoro. He lives beneath the giant camphor tree in the woodland behind our house. I met him too while we were waiting for Dad's bus. He gave us the most incredible gift . . . seeds and acorns wrapped in a bamboo leaf and tied with a ribbon made of grass.

Mei *opens the leaf parcel and seeds and acorns tumble out. She plants the seeds in neat little rows and waters them with a watering can. She sits and waits for the seeds to germinate.*

Satsuki (*letter*)   We have planted the seeds in your garden in front of the house . . . we thought a little forest might grow to give you some shade when you come home. But it's taking too long. Mei watches them all day waiting for them to sprout and it's starting to make her crabby. Here is a picture of Mei as a crab. Mei has drawn you a picture too . . . of Totoro. Please get well soon. Love, Satsuki.

19c – Satsuki's Letter

Nurse   Are they settling into their new home?

Yasuko   Yes . . . I . . . (*Laughs.*)

Nurse   What is it?

Yasuko *holds up a drawing of Totoro that was included in the letter.*

Nurse   Oh my word! Look at that!

The two of them laugh. The laughter is too much for **Yasuko** *and she goes into an uncontrollable coughing fit.*

20a – The Totoro Tree

The sliding doors to the house are open and **Tatsuo** *is making up the girls' futon beds.*

Satsuki *and* **Mei** *watch the flowerbed for signs of growth.*

Mei   It's been days! Why won't they grow?!

Tatsuo   These things take time.

Mei   Do you think they'll sprout tomorrow?

Tatsuo   That sounds like something your new friend would know. (*Finished.*) There we go . . . all done. Time for bed, girls.

Mei *and* **Satsuki** *climb into their beds.* **Tatsuo** *tucks them in.*

Tatsuo   Goodnight, Mei.

Mei   Goodnight.

Tatsuo   Goodnight, Satsuki.

Satsuki   Goodnight, Dad.

Tatsuo *turns off the light. The girls settle down to sleep.* **Tatsuo** *heads to his office to work.*

Night falls.

20b – The Totoro Tree

Night-time.

The house is silent.

Out of the darkness march **Ōtotoro**, **Shōtotoro** *and* **Chōtotoro**. **Ōtotoro** *holds* **Tatsuo**'s *umbrella high above his head.* **Shōtotoro** *and* **Chōtotoro** *carry leaves on long stalks. They march up to the flowerbed. They are performing a ritual, marching to and fro, occasionally bowing to the flowerbed.*

Satsuki *stirs from her sleep. She watches transfixed as the totoros perform their ritual.*

Satsuki (*whispers*)   Mei . . . Mei . . . wake up . . .

Mei (*wakes*)   Huh?

Satsuki (*whispers*)   Shh . . . look . . .!

Mei *joins* **Satsuki** *watch the monsters do their magical dance.* **Mei** *can't contain herself – she rushes to join them.*

Satsuki   Mei! (*Rushes after her.*)

The girls join in the ritual, mimicking the totoros' movements – marching up and down, jumping, raising the umbrella. It's clear that **Ōtotoro** *is exerting himself.*

All of them together – the three totoros and the two girls – stand in a line alongside the flowerbed willing the seeds to germinate, pushing for the acorns to sprout roots and leaves.

It works! Pop – a sprout appears. Pop pop. More sprouts! Pop pop pop. Seedlings appear all over the flowerbed. And still **Ōtotoro** *pushes himself. The seedlings grow and expand, pushing into the air.*

The plants grow higher and higher – creepers spiralling upwards, leaves unfurling, branches reaching into the sky. With every push, with every raise of the umbrella, trees grow higher and higher until it seems everything is tree.

Act Two

1 – Ocarina

High at the top of the magical trees sit **Satsuki**, **Mei**, **Ōtotoro**, **Shōtotoro** *and* **Chōtotoro** – *each one of them has an ocarina. Balanced in the branches, the little band plays out a jaunty tune to the night sky.*

2 – Tree Sprouts

Morning.

Tatsuo *is asleep at his desk. He wakes up, a piece of paper stuck to his face.*

He steps outside into the sun. He walks over to the flowerbed and inspects it – a few tiny, green sprouts poke just above the soil. He smiles.

Tatsuo *walks back to the house and opens the large sliding doors, revealing* **Mei** *and* **Satsuki** *asleep in bed. The girls stir.*

Tatsuo   Wakey-wakey . . .

Satsuki (*sleepy*)   Dad . . .?

Tatsuo   . . . rise and shine . . .

Mei   Huh . . .?

Tatsuo   How did you sleep?

Satsuki (*sees the sprouts in the flowerbed*)   Mei – *look!*

The girls run over to the flowerbed to inspect the tiny shoots.

Mei   Let me see . . . let me see . . .

Satsuki   I thought . . . I thought I'd dreamt . . .

Mei   No – it was *real!*

The girls cheer and dance around the flowerbed in delight.

Tatsuo *looks on – pleased that they are finding some happiness. He looks at his watch and realises if he doesn't act quickly, he's going to miss his bus.*

Tatsuo (*panicked*)   Oh . . . shoot! Girls . . . I need to . . . I need to get going . . . Satsuki, will you fix some breakfast for the two of you?

Satsuki   Yes, Dad.

Tatsuo   You're helping Granny out today . . . be good . . . do as you are told . . . yes?

Satsuki   Yes, Dad.

Mei   Yes, Daddy.

Tatsuo   Okay . . . okay . . . where's my briefcase? Where did I put my notebook? Argh! I need to buy an alarm clock . . .

Mei *finds* **Tatsuo**'s *briefcase and notebook.* **Satsuki** *finds a clean shirt for her father.* **Mei** *opens the briefcase and* **Satsuki** *folds up the shirt to put inside.* **Mei** *also puts in the notebook. They hand the briefcase to* **Tatsuo**.

Satsuki   There's a fresh shirt in there.

Tatsuo   Thank you.

Satsuki   Do you have money for lunch?

Tatsuo (*checks pockets*)   Yes . . . yes, I think so.

Mei   And change for the bus?

Tatsuo   Yes. I do. Thank you, girls. How's my hair?

Mei   Fine.

Satsuki   It's fine.

Tatsuo   Okay. Go next door straight after breakfast. Brush your teeth. Bye, girls! (*Exits.*)

Satsuki *and* **Mei** *wave goodbye.*

Mei   I'm not going to brush my teeth.

Satsuki *puffs herself up like* **Ōtotoro**.

Satsuki *roars.*

Mei *roars back.*

Satsuki *roars even louder.*

Mei   *Doh-doh-ohhh!*

Satsuki   *Doh-doh-ohhh!*

3 – A Telegram

The Ogakis' house.

Kanta *has fixed his model plane and is playing with it carefully.*

Hiroshi *is fixing a bicycle, a toolbox next to him.*

Hiroshi   Can you pass me the spanner . . . the little one . . .?

Kanta *fetches a spanner from the toolbox.*

Hiroshi   How's your aeroplane?

Kanta   It's okay.

Hiroshi   Has the glue set?

Kanta   Yes.

Hiroshi   Good, good. I'm going to raise the seat a little . . . okay?

Kanta *nods.*

Hiroshi   You'll be able to run errands for your mother . . . perhaps I should put a basket on the handlebars . . .?

Kanta   Dad . . .?

Hiroshi   Yes, Kanta?

Kanta   How do you talk to girls?

Hiroshi (*stops*)   Um . . . girls?

Kanta   Yeah.

Hiroshi   How do you talk to them?

Kanta   Yes.

Hiroshi   You talk to them how you would talk to anyone. Come and sit on this thing . . . I want to see if the seat's too high.

Kanta *sits on the bike.*

Hiroshi   Okay?

Kanta *nods.*

Hiroshi   What do you want to say to . . . *girls?*

Kanta   I just want to be friends. But I keep making faces.

Hiroshi   I see. (*Beat.*) I'll tell you what I wish someone had told me when I was your age . . . you are going to grow up really fast . . . you may think that next year, two years, three years, seem forever away . . . but they're not . . . and when you're older you're going to wish that you had been nicer to people . . . that you had spent less time worrying about being embarrassed or getting laughed at . . . and that you had spent more time being honest. Talk to a girl . . . not because you want something from her . . . not because you want her to be your friend . . . but because talking with people, listening to people, telling stories and playing games . . . is simply the best use of your time . . . and spending time with each other, that's where friendships come from. Okay?

Kanta   Okay.

Hiroshi   How's the bike for you?

Kanta   The seat is a bit high.

Hiroshi   Give it a few months . . . it'll be just right.

A knock at the door. A **Postman** *arrives with a telegram in his hand.*

Postman   Hello . . .? Excuse me . . .?

Hiroshi   Yes . . . hello.

Postman   Hi . . . I have a telegram for your neighbours . . .
the Kusakabes . . .? No one's home next door.

Hiroshi   Ah . . . yes . . . of course.

Postman   Can I leave it with you?

Hiroshi   That's fine . . . I'll make sure they get it. (*Takes the
telegram.*)

Postman   Thank you. (*Exits.*)

Hiroshi *goes to put the telegram in his pocket but has a better idea.*

Hiroshi   Are the girls with Granny today?

Kanta   Yes.

Hiroshi   Why don't you deliver this to Satsuki?

4 – Vegetable Patch

The allotment.

Corn, tomato plants and cucumber plants.

Satsuki and **Mei** *are helping* **Granny** *as she picks the ripe fruit
from the plants.*

Granny   Leave the green ones be . . . just a gentle twist and
the ripe ones should pop off.

Satsuki (*picks a tomato*)   Like this?

Granny   That's right. You're a natural gardener. I'll call
you Satsuki Green-Fingers. Now . . . there's a real skill when
it comes to the corn . . . look at this . . . these outer leaves are
the husk . . . and this wispy hair on the top is the silk . . . you
want to pick them when the silk has gone brown but the
husk is still green . . . pull it down . . . give it a twist . . .
(*Breaks off a corncob.*) You girls try.

Satsuki *does so.*

Mei   It's not working!

Granny   Let me see . . . try a little harder . . .

Mei *succeeds.*

Granny   Well done, Mei! That's enough picking for today, I think. Granny needs a sit down.

Satsuki   I've never picked vegetables before.

Granny   These are full of lovely sunshine and vitamins . . . fresh from the vine . . . here . . . take a bite. (*Passes* **Satsuki** *a tomato.*)

Satsuki (*takes a bite*)   It's warm!

Granny   It's been out in the sun all morning! I bet you've never tasted a tomato so fresh before. Mei . . . would you like one? It's very good for you . . . very healthy.

Mei   Healthy?

Granny   Oh yes . . . it'll keep you fit and strong . . . good for what ails you.

Satsuki   We should save some for Mum . . . is that alright, Granny? She's coming home this weekend.

Granny   Is she? Oh that *is* good news.

Satsuki   Not for good . . . just for Saturday and Sunday night . . . the doctor wants her to get used to the new house a little at a time.

Granny   I bet you're looking forward to having your mummy home, eh Mei?

Mei   I'm going to give her this sweetcorn. It's full of vitamins.

Kanta *arrives on his bike.*

Granny   Kanta! Good gracious . . . whatever's the rush?

Kanta (*composes himself, gives a little bow*)   Hello, Satsuki.

Satsuki (*taken aback by his politeness*)   Hi . . . um . . . hello, Kanta.

Granny   What's all this about?

Kanta   A *telegram* . . . for the Kusakabes . . . I thought it might be important. (*Hands it to* **Satsuki**.)

Satsuki   Thank you. Should I open it? Dad won't be home until this evening.

Granny   No one bothers to send a telegram without good reason . . . you had better open it.

Satsuki *opens it and reads.*

Mei   What does it say?

Satsuki   I . . . (*Upset.*)

Granny *takes the telegram.*

Mei   Satsuki . . .?

Granny   Oh . . . I . . .

Mei   What does it say?

Satsuki   Just . . . just to contact the doctor.

Mei   Is Mum okay?

Satsuki   I don't know.

Granny   Do you know your father's number at the university?

Satsuki   I do.

Granny   Good. Kanta – take Satsuki to your aunt's house and ask if she can use her telephone.

Kanta   Okay.

Granny   Satsuki – let your father know what's happened. He'll call the hospital. You'll be able to wait with Kanta for your father to call back.

Satsuki   Okay . . . okay . . .

Granny   Satsuki – everything is going to be fine. You go . . . make the phone call . . . I'll stay with Mei.

Kanta *and* **Satsuki** *exit on the bicycle.*

Mei   I want to go too.

Granny   No, Mei . . . stay here.

Mei   If they go to the hospital, I want to go too.

Granny   You do as you are told.

Mei   Satsuki! Wait for me! (*Runs off, clinging to her sweetcorn.*)

Granny   Mei! Mei!!

5 – The Path of the Wind

Song: 'The Path of the Wind'.

Kanta *and* **Satsuki** *arrive at* **Kanta**'s *aunt's house.* **Kanta** *shows* **Satsuki** *the telephone which hangs on the wall.* **Satsuki** *picks up the handset and speaks.*

Satsuki   Hello? Hi . . . yes . . . I want to make a phone call . . . Tokyo 31-13-82, please . . . (*Waits.*) Hello . . .? My name is Satsuki Kusakabe . . . I need to speak to Professor Kusakabe in the Department of Archaeology . . . I'm his daughter . . . yes . . . tell him it's urgent . . . thank you. (*Waits.*)

Kanta *is watching, supportive.*

Tatsuo *is on the other end of the phone-line in Tokyo.*

Tatsuo (*telephone*)   Hello . . .?

Satsuki   Dad . . .?

Tatsuo (*telephone*)   Satsuki . . .? Is everything alright?

Satsuki   No . . . I don't know . . . I don't think so . . .

Tatsuo (*telephone*)   Tell me what's happened?

Satsuki   A telegram came . . . from the hospital . . . it says we need to call right away . . .

Tatsuo (*telephone*)   Okay.

Satsuki   Has something happened, Dad? Is Mum alright?

Tatsuo (*telephone*)   I'll call the hospital straight away. Where are you now?

Satsuki   I'm at Kanta's aunt's house . . .

Kanta   It's the only telephone in the village.

Satsuki   . . . it's the only phone in the village.

Tatsuo (*telephone*)   Okay . . . is someone with you? Can you stay by the phone?

Satsuki   Yes . . . I . . . I think so.

Tatsuo (*telephone*)   I'm sure there's no reason to worry . . . I'll call the hospital now and then I will ring you back straight away.

Satsuki   Yes, Dad.

Tatsuo (*telephone*)   I need to hang up now.

Satsuki   Okay.

The phone-line goes dead, and **Satsuki** *hangs up the handset.*
Satsuki *is obviously upset with worry.* **Kanta** *tries to comfort her.*

'The Path of the Wind' resumes.

6 – The Goat and the Corn

Mei *is running through the village – she has lost sight of* **Satsuki**.
She cradles the corncob in her arms.

Mei   Satsuki!

No response.

Mei   SATSUKI!! Where are you?!

Her shouting has disturbed a sleeping goat. The goat wakes up and slowly walks towards **Mei**. **Mei** *is frightened.*

Mei   Oh . . . hello, goat.

The goat bleats.

Mei   What do you want? Go away.

The goat bleats.

Mei   You want the sweetcorn . . . is that it?

The goat bleats.

Mei   You can't have it.

The goat bleats.

Mei   No – it's not for you. No.

The goat moves closer.

Mei   Get away! This corn is for my mummy . . . she needs it to make her better.

The goat bleats.

Mei   No! Go away!

Kanta *and* **Satsuki** *arrive on the bicycle, ringing the bicycle's bell and shooing at the goat. The goat snorts and walks away.*

Satsuki   Are you alright?

Mei   Stupid goat wanted the corn.

Satsuki   Let's go home.

Mei   Did you speak to Daddy?

Satsuki   I did.

Mei   What did he say? Did he speak to the doctor?

Satsuki   Yes.

Mei   What did he say?!

Satsuki   Mum is sick.

Mei   But she's getting better.

Satsuki   No. She's not. She's getting worse. She needs rest.

Mei   She can sleep in my bed.

Satsuki   She's not coming home, Mei . . . not this weekend or anytime soon. She needs rest . . . she needs doctors . . . she needs quiet . . . she's not going to get that at home with you climbing all over her . . . trying to play with her . . . feeding her your stupid corn . . .

Mei   It's not stupid.

Satsuki   Mum is very sick . . . and if the stress . . . if the effort . . . of getting her from the hospital to the house . . . is going to hurt her . . .

Mei   But I want her to meet Totoro.

Satsuki   She could die, Mei. She could die.

Satsuki *exits*.

Mei *is very upset*.

Kanta   Hey . . . um . . . everything's going to be okay . . .

Mei (*quietly*)   I hate her.

Kanta   What . . .?

Mei   I hate her. She's so mean. (*Cries*.)

Kanta *tries to comfort her*.

Kanta   Hey . . . um . . . come on . . . I'll walk you home.

7a – Granny is Here to Help

The Kusakabe house.

Mei *is inside, curled up on her futon bed.*

Satsuki *sits with her legs hanging off the veranda.*

Granny *is tidying up, picking up laundry and generally trying to be as helpful as she can.*

Granny   Why don't you help me put away this laundry. You know where it goes better than I.

Satsuki   Just leave it.

Granny   I don't mind helping out. Now tell me where your father's underpants live and whether or not you'd like your socks rolled into a ball.

Silence.

Satsuki   Thank you.

Granny   You're very welcome, my dear. (*Beat.*) Your father should have arrived at the hospital by now.

Satsuki   I guess.

Granny   I'm sure seeing him will make your mother feel much better.

Satsuki (*sigh*)

Granny   All this worry over a silly little cold. She'll be fine in no time . . . she may even be able to reschedule her visit for next weekend . . .

Satsuki   She's not coming home.

Granny   No?

Satsuki   Not next weekend . . . probably not anytime soon . . .

Granny   Why do you say that?

Satsuki *shrugs.*

Granny   We all get colds and we all shake them off.

Satsuki   When she first got sick . . . they said it was just a little cold . . . that she would get better in a few days . . . she's been in hospital ever since.

Granny   That doesn't mean . . .

Satsuki   What if she dies?

Granny *is speechless.*

Satsuki   What if . . . what if they're not telling the truth . . . what if she's already dead?

Granny   Satsuki . . . I'm sure . . .

Satsuki   Please don't lie to me, Granny . . . I couldn't take it . . . I just couldn't.

Granny (*comforts* **Satsuki**)   Hey . . . now . . . come here . . . don't say such things . . . don't cry . . . it's alright . . . Granny's here . . .

Mei *stands in the doorway. It is clear that she has heard every word. She carries the sweetcorn. A determined look comes across her face. She finds her sandals and slips them on. She exits – headed to the hospital and her mother.*

7b – Granny is Here to Help

Satsuki *and* **Granny** *are searching for* **Mei** *– they can't find her anywhere.*

Satsuki   Mei?!

Granny   Mei?!

Satsuki   It's not funny anymore, Mei!

Granny   Come on now, Mei . . . where are you hiding?!

Satsuki   Mei?!

Granny   I don't understand it . . . where else could she be
. . .?

Satsuki   It's my fault.

Granny   How is it your fault?

Satsuki   I shouted at her this morning . . . I shouted at her
. . . and now . . . and now she . . . if anything has happened
to her . . .

Granny   Shush now . . . she's just hiding out in the trees . . .
or she's looking for the soot-sprites . . .

Kanta *enters, running.*

Kanta   She's not at the bus stop . . . I didn't see her
anywhere on the road.

Satsuki   She's taken the corn.

Kanta   She wouldn't have gone to the hospital, would she?

Satsuki   She must've done.

Granny   No . . . that's too long of a walk . . . it's too far to
walk even for an adult.

Satsuki   I don't know where else she would've gone. I have
to find her . . . I have to . . . Granny . . .?

Granny   Stay here . . . I can't be responsible for losing you
both.

Satsuki   No . . . I'm sorry . . . I'm sorry . . . (*Runs off.*)

Granny   Satsuki!!

Kanta   Should I go after her?

Granny   No . . . run home . . . run and find your father . . .
tell him that Mei's gone missing . . . tell him we need all the
help we can get.

8 – Lost Child

Song: 'Lost Child'.

Satsuki *is searching for* **Mei** *along the road. She calls out to a* **Farmer** *who is reaping wheat in a field.*

Satsuki   Excuse me . . .? Hello . . .?

Farmer   Hello there!

Satsuki   You haven't seen a little girl come by this way . . . a little girl with pigtails . . .?

Farmer   I can't say I have.

Satsuki   She would've been a carrying some corn . . .?

Farmer   A little girl carrying corn . . .?

Satsuki   That's right.

Farmer   I'm afraid not.

Satsuki   Are you sure?

Farmer   I've been out here all day . . . I would've noticed.

Satsuki   Okay. I'll try the other road. Thank you for your time. Mei . . . Mei . . .?!

Satsuki *runs out into the road – into the path of an oncoming motorcycle-with-sidecar. She waves it down. Riding the motorbike is a* **Man***, in the sidecar is a* **Woman***.*

Man   Are you insane?! What are you doing?!

Satsuki   I'm sorry . . .

Man   You can't just run out into the road like that!

Satsuki   I'm sorry, but . . . have you seen . . . my little sister . . . have you seen a girl come this way?

Woman   Your sister?

Satsuki   Her name is Mei . . .

Woman   Oh my . . . is she lost?

Satsuki (*nods*)   She may be trying to get to the hospital.

Man   I haven't seen a little girl . . . have you?

Woman   No. We just came from the hospital . . . we would've seen her if she took this road.

Man   I'm sorry . . . we haven't seen anything.

Satsuki   Okay . . . thank you for your time.

Woman   Wait! Which village are you from?

Satsuki   Matsugo.

Man   That's a long way for anyone . . . your younger sister?

Satsuki   She can be very determined.

Kanta *arrives on his bicycle.*

Kanta   Satsuki!

Satsuki   Have you found her?

Kanta   My dad's got the whole village looking for her . . . I'll ride on to the hospital . . . you should head back home. Satsuki . . . they're searching the pond.

Silence.

Satsuki (*turns to the couple*)   Excuse me . . . but could I trouble you? I need to get back to my village.

Man   Yes . . . yes, of course . . . I . . .

The **Woman** *gets out of the sidecar.*

Woman   Here . . . you take my seat . . . my husband will take you to Matsugo.

Satsuki   Thank you. You're very kind.

Woman *helps* **Satsuki** *into the sidecar.*

Woman   I'll start walking home . . . if you need to join the search . . .

Man   Of course.

Satsuki   Thank you.

The **Man** *and* **Satsuki** *drive off.* **Kanta** *gets on his bicycle and heads to the hospital.*

9 – A Sandal in the Village Pond

The **Villagers** *have gathered, including* **Hiroshi**, **Tsukiko** *and* **Miss Hara**. *They are dredging the pond with long poles of bamboo.* **Granny** *is on her knees to one side, her hands clasped together around a single sandal but also in prayer.*

Hiroshi   The mud is deeper at that end . . .

Villager One   Have we got any more bamboo poles?

Villager Two   It's getting dark . . . we need more light . . .

Hiroshi   Work in a circular motion . . . be methodical!

The **Man** *and* **Satsuki** *arrive on the motorbike.* **Satsuki** *leaps out of the sidecar and runs to the pond. She is caught by* **Tsukiko**.

Satsuki   Mei!

Tsukiko   Satsuki . . . stop.

Satsuki   Mei . . . is she . . . is she in there . . .?

Tsukiko   We don't know . . .

Miss Hara   Satsuki . . .

Satsuki   Miss Hara! What's going on? What are they doing?

Miss Hara   Someone from the search party . . . we were all looking for your sister . . . they found a sandal in the water . . .

Tsukiko   Hiroshi . . . Satsuki's here.

Hiroshi (*shouts*)   Everybody stop what you're doing! The sister is here.

Tsukiko   Where's the sandal . . .?

Granny   I have it . . . I have it . . .

Satsuki   Granny . . . is it hers . . .?

Granny   I don't know . . . I can't say . . . here . . . look . . .

Silence as **Satsuki** *inspects the sandal. The silence is sickening.*

Satsuki   It's not hers.

Granny   Oh thank goodness.

Tsukiko   Are you sure?

Satsuki   It's not Mei's . . . it's not hers!

Hiroshi   It's not her sandal! Stop dredging!

Villager One   It's not the little girl's?

Villager Two   Thank heavens for that.

Villager Three   So where is she?

Hiroshi   We're not done yet . . . there's still a little girl missing.

Villager Two   It's getting dark . . . we need light.

Tsukiko   Go home . . . get torches . . . change out of your wet clothes if you need to . . . we'll start searching the fields in half an hour!

The **Villagers** *disperse.*

Satsuki   They won't find her.

Granny   We'll have the whole village looking for her. She'll turn up somewhere. I'm certain of it.

Satsuki   It's cold . . . she'll be frightened . . .

Granny   Let's get you home . . . wait for news . . .

Satsuki *wrestles away from* **Granny** *and runs away.*

Granny   Satsuki! SATSUKI!!

10a – Looking for Totoro

At the base of the huge camphor tree.

Satsuki *pushes through the tangle of the forest and collapses at the base of the tree.*

Satsuki   Please . . . can you hear me . . .? Mei has gone missing . . . my little sister . . . she's out there on the road alone . . . it's getting dark . . . you have to help me . . . you have to help her . . . please . . . you're supposed to protect us . . . aren't supposed to protect us . . .?

She falls to her knees, weeping.

Please . . . Totoro . . .

From the roots of the tree appears **Shōtotoro**. *He looks at the crying* **Satsuki**. *He makes a little whistle and* **Chōtotoro** *appears from behind the tree. They look at* **Satsuki**, *knowing that they have to help.* **Chōtotoro** *takes the initiative and approaches* **Satsuki**.

Satsuki   Hello . . . can you take me to Totoro?

Chōtotoro *gives the nod to his brother.* **Shōtotoro** *gives a little psychic exertion and the roots of the tree unfurl, revealing the entrance to the totoros' burrow.*

Led by **Chōtotoro** *and* **Shōtotoro**, **Satsuki** *enters the burrow beneath the camphor tree.*

10b – Looking for Totoro

Satsuki *falls through the roots of the ancient tree and lands with a bump in the dark, hollowed-out cavity beneath.*

Satsuki   Totoro . . . Totoro, please . . . it's me, Satsuki . . . you have to help . . . Mei has gone missing . . . our mother is

very sick and . . . and I think Mei has gone to the hospital to
see her . . . but she's not on the road . . . people are looking
everywhere for her . . . the whole village . . . in the fields . . .
in the henhouses . . . even at the bottom of the pond . . .
please . . . I can't lose her . . . I was supposed to look after
her . . . I was supposed to be strong . . . I'm her big sister . . .
but I shouted at her and she ran away . . . I can't . . . please
. . . it's dark and cold . . . she'll be frightened . . . (*Cries.*)

Ōtotoro *appears.*

Ōtotoro   *Doh-doh-ohhh.*

Satsuki *steps back, a little frightened.*

Satsuki   Please, Totoro . . . I don't know what else to do.

Ōtotoro *fills his lungs – his chest puffs out like the throat of a
frigatebird. He opens his mouth as wide as it can go and lets out an
enormous bellowing roar.*

Satsuki *covers her ears.*

Ōtotoro *stops and listens but is only met with silence. He fills his
lungs once more and lets out a second enormous roar.*

Again he stops and listens. **Satsuki** *listens too.*

In the distance comes the reply. A meow.

*Thundering over the landscape, racing through fields, leaping from
treetop to treetop comes the* **Catbus**. *MEOW-ZOOM-WHOOSH!*

Ōtotoro *looks down to* **Satsuki** *as if to say: everything will be
alright.*

The **Catbus** *lands heavily, but gracefully, next to* **Satsuki** *and*
Ōtotoro. *A big grin across* **Ōtotoro**'s *face.*

The **Catbus** *looks to* **Satsuki** *as if to say: how can I help you?*
Ōtotoro *gives her a little nudge.*

Satsuki   Take me to my sister . . .?

The destination plate on the **Catbus** *changes from 'FOREST' to 'MEI'. The door opens in the side of the* **Catbus**.

Satsuki   Thank you!

Satsuki *climbs onboard the* **Catbus**. *With a great yowling mewl, the* **Catbus** *leans back on its haunches and bounds away.*

Ōtotoro *raises one of his big paws in farewell.*

Ōtotoro   *Doh-doh-ohhh!*

11 – Mei is Missing

A dark country road.

A row of Jizō statues along the wayside – the guardian of children and travellers.

Mei, *tired and dirty, clings to her corncob as she shelters by the statues. She is scared and alone. She is scratching on the husk of the corn with a stick – writing something. Her task finished, she looks up to the sky.*

Mei   I'm sorry I ran away, Satsuki. I'm cold. I don't even know which way I came . . . the way home . . . (*Beat.*) I want my mummy.

She settles down to sleep – using the corncob as a pillow.

Out of the shadows, from behind the statues, come the **Soot-Sprites**. *They swirl around the statues silently. They gather together and cover* **Mei** *like a sooty, black blanket – keeping her warm.*

A 'meow' in the distance.

Mei *stirs. The* **Soot-Sprites** *disperse.*

The **Catbus** *arrives – its headlight-eyes glowing brilliantly. The door opens and out steps* **Satsuki**.

Satsuki   Mei!

The sisters embrace.

Mei (*tears*)   I'm sorry . . . I'm so sorry . . .

Satsuki   The whole village has been looking for you . . . I shouldn't have shouted . . . I'm just so glad you're okay.

The **Catbus** *meows.*

Satsuki *strokes the* **Catbus** *between its eyes. The* **Catbus** *purrs.*

Mei *pats the* **Catbus** *on the nose. The* **Catbus** *lets out a little sneeze.*

Mei *is still cradling the corn.*

Satsuki   What's this?

Mei   Vegetables are good for you. Good for your health.

Satsuki   For Mummy?

Mei *nods.*

The **Catbus** *meows. The destination plate changes once again, from 'MEI' to 'HOSPITAL'.*

Satsuki   You'll take us to the hospital? (*To* **Mei**.) Shall we?

Mei   Yes!

The two girls hug the **Catbus**. *The door opens and the two girls get on board.*

12 – Catbus

The **Catbus** *runs across the countryside, down roads, through avenues of trees, along walls, through fields.*

It runs through the search parties out looking for **Mei**.

It runs by cars on the roads, freight trucks and motorcycles.

The **Catbus** *gets into a race with a train, overtaking it easily.*

It crosses the rice fields and villages, up and down the sides of buildings and the trunks of trees.

It passes the **Man** *on the motorbike reuniting with the* **Woman**.

It passes the **Farmer** *in his field.*

The **Catbus** *scampers up an electricity pylon, arching blue electricity crackles down its whiskers. Sparks fly as the* **Catbus** *speeds along the power cables between pylons.*

All the while **Mei** *and* **Satsuki** *peer out into the world – thrilled at it all.*

13a – I'm So Glad

Shichikokuyama Tuberculosis Hospital.

Yasuko *sits up in bed.* **Tatsuo** *sits with her.*

It is a hot night and the window is open.

Yasuko   They shouldn't have bothered you . . . not for a stupid little cold . . . for some blocked-up sinuses and a runny nose . . .

Tatsuo   How are you feeling now?

Yasuko   I'm fine. (*Beat.*) Though it is nice to see you. I've missed your face. (*Beat.*) And I miss the girls.

Tatsuo   We'll all come and visit you this weekend . . . and when they see you in person . . . when they see you smiling and chatting . . . they'll be fine.

Yasuko   I hope so. I hate that I'm missing out on their games and their imaginations and their stories.

Tatsuo   The kids understand . . . more than you'd think.

Yasuko   They shouldn't have to.

Tatsuo   You just need to concentrate on getting better.

Yasuko   Mei sent me a picture of a monster.

Tatsuo   That would be our neighbour – he lives beneath the huge tree behind the house.

Yasuko And you're tucking them in . . . and you're making their breakfast . . . and you're reading to them at night . . . and you're washing their clothes and mending the holes when they get torn . . .?

Tatsuo Yes . . . mostly. I mean . . . I've had help. (*Beat.*) We've made it this far. Just a little further.

Yasuko They put such a brave face on it all . . . Satsuki especially . . . she's at that age . . . hurrying to grow up . . . wanting to be strong . . . and I just want to tell her to slow down. You try to shield them from this . . . all of this . . . hospitals . . . sickness . . . worry . . .

Tatsuo Don't . . . it's okay.

Yasuko And you're hugging them . . . and you're encouraging them . . . and they know how proud we are of them?

Tatsuo Of course. Of course.

Yasuko Because if I get worse . . .

Tatsuo You'll beat this . . . and you'll come home . . . and Mei and Satsuki will run you ragged with stories of monsters and creatures in the forest.

Yasuko Tell me about their friends. Tell me about totoro.

Tatsuo He's big and furry and he smells of mud . . . and he lets out a big roar like this: ROARRR!!

Yasuko *and* **Tatsuo** *are laughing together – they are happy. This is the first good laugh they've shared in ages.*

13b – I'm So Glad

Looking in through the hospital window, in the branches of a tree, are **Mei**, **Satsuki** *and the* **Catbus**. **Mei** *still clings to the sweetcorn.*

Mei Look . . .

Satsuki   I can see.

Mei   She's laughing.

Satsuki   Yes.

Mei   They're both laughing.

13c – I'm So Glad

Yasuko *shivers.*

Tatsuo   Are you getting cold?

Tatsuo *goes to close the window, but he finds* **Mei***'s corncob on the outside sill.*

Tatsuo   Huh.

Yasuko   What is it?

Tatsuo *shows her the sweetcorn.*

There is a message scratched onto the husk.

Yasuko (*reads*)   'For Mummy . . . get well soon.'

13d – I'm So Glad

Satsuki   We should get home . . . Granny will be worried.

Mei   Okay.

Satsuki   Mum's going to be alright.

Mei   I know.

Satsuki   Everything's going to be alright.

The girls hug.

14 – My Neighbour Totoro

The Kusakabe house.

The **Catbus** *arrives and* **Mei** *and* **Satsuki** *are finally home.*

The **Catbus** *meows, climbs to the roof of the house, and smiles down on the two girls. They wave as the* **Catbus** *gently fades from sight – its brilliant eyes and teeth the last things to disappear from view.*

An exhausted **Granny** *comes out of the house having heard voices.*

Mei *runs up to* **Granny** *and gives her the biggest hug.*

Kanta *exits the house – he also relieved to see the girls returned. He waves meekly at* **Satsuki**.

A moment between the two young friends.

Everyone heads inside the house.

Out of the bushes come **Shōtotoro**, **Chōtotoro** *and* **Ōtotoro** *– parading up and down, leaves and umbrella in the air. They have clearly been observing and are glad that the girls are home safely. They stop in front of the house and bring out their ocarinas. They begin to play.*

Song: 'My Neighbour Totoro'.

For a complete listing of
Methuen Drama titles, visit:
www.bloomsbury.com/drama

Follow us on Twitter and keep up to date
with our news and publications
@MethuenDrama